For Salty and Pam —

Across the miles, across
the years. Thanks for
your friendship and support.

Michael Winter

4 October 2009

The
British Detective

poems by

Michael Wurster

MAIN STREET RAG PUBLISHING COMPANY
CHARLOTTE, NORTH CAROLINA

Library of Congress Control Number: 2009929540

ISBN 13: 978-159948-190-6

Produced in the United States of America

Main Street Rag
PO Box 690100
Charlotte, NC 28227
www.MainStreetRag.com

Acknowledgements:

Some of the poems in this collection have appeared in the following publications:

5 AM, The Antigonish Review, Bogg, Caprice, The Comstock Review, Edgz, The Endless Mountains Review, The Exchange, Figurative Language: Image & Metaphor, HEArt Quarterly, Iodine Poetry Journal, Janus Head, The Main Street Rag, The Old Red Kimono, Penny Dreadful, Pittsburgh City Paper, Pittsburgh Post-Gazette, The Pittsburgh Quarterly, Pleiades, Poemata, Poems-For-All, Poet Lore, SAE Communique, The South Pittsburgh Reporter, Strong Winds, and *yawp.*

Contents

Michael Wurster

Special thanks to:
Joan Bauer, James Deahl, Ziggy Edwards,
Romella Kitchens, and Judith Robinson.

GUNFIRE BREAKS THE SILENCE

A landscape,
flat mountains multiplying backwards,
broken towns like castoff shells under the sky.

The dead artist sprawled
under a cactus tree at the edge of the town.

Scrawled on his tablet:
"I enclose and possess all creation
—open my doors!"

In the distance
near the horizon,
horsemen riding away.

NEWSBOY

Newsboy
in his fifties
with wild hair
and gray clothing

shivering on the corner
of Fifth and Wood,
hands in pockets,
whistling

"Saint Louis Blues"
out of tune.

WELFARE: INTAKE

(Saw the papers in
the morning oh god
and they were the
same as the evening
papers were yesterday
and will be again at
five o' clock.)

BEGIN:

and we will see signs and truths
and we will see fear behind your eyes
we will see that you have been between
the sun and the minotaur

are now
between the stink of failure
                    and the sweat of
                                death

.

("We are priests
insofar as we
administer the
sacraments of our
civilization.")

NEXT:

STATION WAGON

1.

The lights

went on
and off
at will.

2.

The back

littered with
broken bottles

flotsam/jetsam.

3.

It was magnetic

and when
an airplane
passed over

it lifted
ever so gently
from the road.

Michael Wurster

LAST REUNION

1. The Approach

Her apartment
was in a forgotten quarter
of the city.

I remembered a gray landscape,
dark and voracious birds.

2. Divertissement

She served cookies
and flavored tea.

The talk was desultory and tentative,
both embracing and avoiding the past.

3. Two Pictures

In the first, the knight stands at the
side of the road looking up at the lady.
He is emaciated, his armor rusted and
dirty. She is astride a big white horse.
Her long blue-black hair. Behind her is
a dwarf on a pony.

The second recapitulates the first,
but for the addition of a cockatoo
and a small dog.

4. The End

She turned the third card:
the visionary company of death,
their hollow singing eyes.

The fury of their singing fills the room.

THE PRINCE

I have left my own country.
My mother the queen weeps,

my father the king
has sent an assassin behind me.

Those walls and towers
are closed forever.

Nothing more exists save
the wolves on the mountain,

and your gray eyes
before me like a dream.

PERU

The beach is white and narrow,
as wide as from that wall to that wall
and behind it the jungle.

An old weather-beaten
cabana and several shacks. We'll need
pontoons on our plane. There's
no road.

You're worried about mosquitoes?

Worry about anacondas. Great snakes.
They drop from trees, crush you
and eat you whole.

You ask how I know about this place?

Michael Wurster

PITTSBURGH IS MY CITY

1.

Pat and I are in O'Rourke's;
we're not married yet.

Through the big window
I see John Metcalfe pass by,
hail him in.

John tells us he's been promoted,
a poet supervising 27 people!

I get John to tell Pat
the story about Henry Miller and the duck,
a Paris story.

2.

We drop John at Oakland Square, turn
down Fifth Avenue toward the Birmingham
Bridge. It is a cold January night.
My car is a dark color, dark blue,
an Oldsmobile.

This is my city. I am at home here.

RETURN TO CAPE MAY

From Room 214,
The Jetty Motel,
Overlooking the Atlantic

I think of Canute,
or was it Alfred?

throne-borne,
carried by his men
down to the sea's side,

commanded, "Roll on!"
and by god it did,
thus legitimizing the king.

It still rolls on.

Count: benches
on the promenade,
a blue beach house,
a rowboat lettered "Cape May,"
a lifeguard chair, a
red/green/and white beach umbrella.

There is a hazy sky.
It is hot.
A few sun bathers
dare the water,
still cold in June,
with their toes.

Count: sea birds,
gulls or terns,
with their distinctive cry.

Michael Wurster

They are the true
ghosts of this place,
if ghosts there be.

GEOPOLITICS IN NOVEMBER

Walking from my car:
a plastic cup
rattling across an empty street
in the wind.

I thought of the Orientals—
Basho, etc.,
how they would find

significance in this.

Michael Wurster

AMERICAN LITERATURE

Finally,

a stranger
at the end
of the bar

scanned us all
and,
apropos of nothing,

said:

"a lot of people
felt that way
about Mexico,

but when they got there,
all they did was drink
and die."

QUIET HOUSE

In a quiet house at night
you can hear the cat
eating dry food in the kitchen.

Even in the city
you can hear the summer locusts.

In a quiet house at night
on a small street
with silent parked cars,

you think of waking your wife
for sex, but don't.

There's enough of it.

Civilization is made possible
by this courtesy.

Michael Wurster

HYPERBOLE . . . OR NOTORIETY?

Like my first wife, who said,
"Michael, to you everything is bizarre."

and "It ain't necessarily so!"

or as Curt DeBor
when I spotted
Nicky Gatalski
lurching up Forbes Avenue:

"Michael, just because you know them
doesn't necessarily mean they're famous."

At the picnic
you said you agreed
with this.

(This is a problem I have,
dramatizing my life.

Thank you.)

THE CORPORATION

1.

It was some force, I won't say spirit,
entered the humans and animals

and changed them.
Much fighting of a terrible nature.

We hired a British detective,
but he soon disappeared.

2.

The young ship's captain
was interested only in his marriage.

3.

After the reception,
the protagonist walked home alone.

He thought about the young captain
and the angry clan leaders,

each nailing the symbol of his clan
to the wall.

The lights along the boardwalk
competed with the light of the moon

on the water.
There was no one around.

Michael Wurster

THAT HARSH WINTER

Through the afternoon
while I slept
you wrote and drew
on the frosted living room
windows
with your finger.

Dieter had already moved
to Marchand Street
where he froze.

That night
Minutello's was like
an end of the world party.
All the restaurants
were closed
except in hotels.

Later in the bar
at Howard Johnson's
you and Anna Marie talked;
I watched the Golden Globe Awards
and Raymond Burr
on the big screen.

Our lives were so tentative then.

ANGELA AND GIZMO

"Hey, you don't trifle with
hearts on the South Side.
Maybe in Lincoln Place or
North Side, but not here."

He waited for her
to return home
to 16th Street
and shot her once
in the head.

Now Angela's in the hospital
and Gizmo's on the loose.

Angela's in the hospital;
she'll be a celebrity if she lives.

Angela's in the hospital
and her Uncle Lee's got a gun.

He's stalking Gizmo
thru the streets and alleys
of the South City.

A guy in the coffee shop says,
"They were such lovebirds a year ago.
They bought balloons for each other at the Giant Eagle."

Michael Wurster

MATURE LOVE

"Because I cannot hope
to turn again."
- T. S. Eliot

The peasants
up to their elbows,
up to their shins
in muck,

and I,
an animal artist
on the empty road
to Warsaw.

"I'm an animal artist,"
I said.
The smell of jasmine
rode the air.

We found a gulley
near some bushes.
I laid down a canvas.
Planes flew overhead.

LIBERATING THE DEATH CAMP

When we liberated the death camps
we made soup.

The people they were starved,
they had not eaten,
they were like cadavers.
They gathered around the soup.

It was good soup,
it had meat
and all kinds of vegetables
--potatoes, carrots, onions.
Steam rose from the big kettle.

The people they gathered around the soup,
but they would not eat, they were afraid,
they had been so long without food.
They were afraid to eat the soup.

It was almost as if
they would rather continue starving,
it was more comfortable for them.

You're doing fine, I admire you,
you're doing a wonderful job,
I know it's not easy,
but I wish you would take the spoon
and hold on.

Please, for my sake as well as yours,
eat the soup.

Michael Wurster

THE MURAL

It was like a cave of snow.
He sat there with a cup of coffee
and an ashtray, the snow
filling the room.

He remembered the turning of the leaves,
as the falling ashes from his cigarette
filled the room as if it were a cave
of dirty snow.

The coffee cup grew hotter in his hand
and a mural bright as candy rose
upon the wall behind his head.

THE AUTHOR

Remembering the shot
that seemed to burst
with no warning
in the back street.

I was proud,
shops on my one side,
supertankers and half-day boats
on the other.

This was a California
that never emerged
from the waves.
Some canyons,

passage of human hours,
a bird or a stone in flight.
I saw the movie. I wrote the book.

Michael Wurster

THE PICNIC

I was on a picnic with friends
down by the river

and I saw a woman who resembled you
in the water. She was wading

and I wanted to be with her
rather than with them,

and I wanted to be with you
rather than with her. Yes.

There were the geese and ducks.
The sun shone and a breeze blew

something that was like goosedown
from the trees, lots of boats out on the water,

and I wanted to be with you.

LANGUAGE

1.

I asked him, the bird.
"I saw you fight against the wind."
Many of them came, a herd of them
by the pool. "Let the nervous creatures
go."

Our mouths speak the truth,
like wings spread across the wood.
A cicada convinced a thousand,
the trumpeter was in front, the chariots
behind.

2.

We are leaves on the trees of all
that is pure. How I love the current,
it hurries and turns up. The image

of the hunter comes in sleep, whitely
drifting companions. The words lie
huge like dead kings on the plain.

Michael Wurster

CHILDREN AT PLAY

1.

The children pose.
Some hold the python,
others the saws and axes.

The next page: their limbs splayed flat.
Blues and greens spoil the picture.
The garden of God contains a secret honey.

2.

The children walk on the ice,
keep their thoughts to themselves.
Rat-tat-tat! Rat-tat-tat!
They fall down brilliantly.

Torn pages wipe the milky mouths;
the real hand waves goodbye again.

BRIGADIER JEFFERSON C. DAVIS

I killed Bull Nelson in Louisville in 1862. He
insulted me in the lobby of the Galt House while
I was in the company of the governor of Indiana.

Nelson gave me the back of his hand, and as he went
up the stairs, I went from bystander to bystander
asking for a weapon. A certain Captain Gibson obliged.
"I always carry the article," he said, producing it
from under his coat.

As I started up the stairs Gibson called after me,
"It's a tranter trigger. Work light." When Nelson
turned from Buell's door and started toward me, I knew
what to do. "Not another step farther!" I cried,
then shot the big man in the chest at a range of about
eight feet.

I was denied promotion for two years, but when Sherman
needed me for Georgia I was ready. They said I had
the eyes of a killer. I rolled up Dan Govan's Arkansas
brigade at Jonesboro like a sheet of paper.

Michael Wurster

LANDSCAPE WITH GRAVESTONES

from a photograph
by Sue Cuenca

That second week I walked among the reeds,
forgetting the other travelers, stroking
the old gravestones: flagrant, by consent
or by force. Dead stars under the ground,

a black and white photograph. The trees
and the buildings carry on a continuous
conversation, the horizon flung somewhere
beyond the spires. It's Lent.

The first fight I had with my lover ended
like this: the erect nipple over the stove,
hand on the spoon stirring the stew, all
the sweet things, sex and kitchen, woman.

There they nurse the sick, in that building.
In a while the stars will appear to soak up
the twilight.

OUBLIETTE

He carried his gift up the three steps
to the rented canoe. He could live
with mother's dying, dead, he said.

The poplar leaves whispered;
the maker's initials were engraved
on the gift, and the inscription:

"Out of want, Out of darkness." A seed
on the tongue. "I missed you when I came
to visit." "Why didn't you just phone?"

Memory resurrects no one. What a joke.
A canoe, then a bus. Clichés make it
no better. The tears formed, the fish

were eaten. Plainsong, call and response.
I laughed my head off as he disappeared
around the bend of the river.

Michael Wurster

THE WRESTLERS

1.

From a gull's oily breath,
the mantra repeats:
give back my browns.

A young girl's interest twice burned.
Her face rescues me, smothering
acute sensations from rawness of emotion.

She sings. The gull flies away.

2.

Everybody is dead
and trembling in a corner.
Savage and brutal men
are not handsome.

They cannot remember the opera.
They would not recommend love.

SALLY

Hot girls are sweet in the summertime.
Sally Reynolds was not hot. Cool.
Slender. Long blonde hair. Black
bathing suit. Not particularly tanned.

Brushing her hair out on the raft,
the hair that never got wet. How
did she get to the raft? Brushing
and brushing. Sweet lassitude.

Cool girl out on the raft at Broomall Lake.
Brushing her hair. Oh, how we spent
our summers.

Michael Wurster

TOWER OF SKULLS

The harrowed fields laugh. Alive. Skinned.
Children lick the letters of their names.
The woman leads us to an invisible canal.

Something cooks in a black iron skillet.
The qualities of rage and hatred. The
cook wears a yellow leather coat, recites

the recipes all night long, yet the food
will be untouched. There is a punishment.
The megaliths bleed unto the fields. The

canal accepts boats, gladly.

RED WINDOW

A universe of food, refrigerator
so full the orange juice
spills out all over the floor.
Not just once.

You prepare too much food.
Shwimps, even feesh.

You wear your clothes so well.
I am your captive. I am your captive
especially when you are naked.

When I was away,
my brother threw his shoe
through the window
out into the snow.

I wish it had been there
when I returned in the Spring.

In our love and hunger,
the perfect body of two ascends.

Michael Wurster

THE AFTERNOON NAP

A woman sits in her kitchen
in her village. Two young boys
have come home to die. The fields
are the graves, a sign nailed
to a tree commanding silence.

A woman sits in her car,
new skin, radiant eyes.
Her heart is pink candy.
A runner zips past. The
instructions get louder and louder,
color follows color.

Each woman puts a finger to her lips,
but there is no one. I take an afternoon nap,
lying beside you. Someone.

DALI'S TURN

Flies settle on the toothless gums
of the overturned bridges. Among
thick lowering clouds many ears dance
on the sand. Yellow shadows cut the eyes.

Bill Weiner plays "Spanish Fandango."
Blind Blake and Boss Crump dance
on the margin. Mothers with babies
at their breasts. Eggs exhibit wonder.

The horizon comes down, extinguishing
the fiery columns.

Michael Wurster

VIRGINIA

Honeycomb: perfection of form.

Raw flesh. Burning.
A black pool full of black water.
A pound of hamburger buried in the dark.

The whole thing was ennobling,
its quivering carcass, its longdrawn death
coughing out our used-up names.

We stood in a blizzard
near Spotsylvania Courthouse,
my mother and I, calling
"Laady, Laaady!"

The fire of childhood, unhealed scars
bolted with life. I told him
if he ever hit me like that again
I'd kill him.

ANGELS IN AMERICA

You in a tinny nickel-dime light,
fuzzy haired, red lipped, cigarette dangling.
Inside an inner light cancels the outer dark.
Blue. Universal. Spectre of all visions.

I come in on a cloud of dust.
You remain the sky behind the thunderhead.
Stromboli. You scream in anger,
remembrance. It becomes theatrical.
Attracting attention is what we live for.

We bed down, rise up, bow to the footlights.
Eyes like locomotives: the futility
of prairies and lost little towns. A
terrible succession of images. The sky
looks full of clouds. Everything bled white.

Michael Wurster

THE ESTATE

Consider the landscape in winter:
not waking up, no break of day.

Something is fulfilled that you never noticed.
Nothing is foreign that you don't already have.

And deep in the eye, gray from the pull
of what must come next, the angry fields.

Room temperature preserves the flow.
Local beasts eat their kill by the shore.

Whatever comes your way here,
don't listen. Whatever listens, divest.

The body is a ghetto. The cook
has forty years invested. The expectant air

calls you back.

THE MOTORCYCLIST

Horn. Then gave me the finger
in my rear view mirror. I must
have almost wiped him out. He'll
be dead on the highway before we meet again.

Dieter's come back from Poland. That boy's
not happy anywhere.

Michael Wurster

MUSEUM QUALITY

Knowingly above the mantel a portrait,
woman smoking a cigarette, too hard
to be beautiful. Each one healed.
Snakes slithered down the switchbacks.

He stuck his tongue out like a god.
They dug him up in the British Isles
or some old German drinking song/vessel
with a handle, you drink out of it.

That hour is passed. The sun
was a chieftain. We buried our enemies
upside down. One thing to the proud.
When hurt he curled like a mouse.

Happy parrots flew over a gorge.
Supernal parrots. Angels. Religion
returned or revived. Present when
we don't expect them, absent

when we do. I can do, right up
to the door and ask to be let in.
A tune at the base of the skull.
I saw something moving in the dust.

The dancing schoolmasters pass by again,
across the lawn and down the road.

CORPSE AND MIRROR

The mechanical man bows
beneath the crystal chandelier.
Those who do not behave
are discarded. The gravediggers

lower the chariot gently,
as if they have always loved
its occupant, a parent or favorite mistress.
A pulse of expectation is followed

by a need. The mechanical woman
stops to talk. The porcelain glaze
of noon filters in. The mechanical man
picks at his dinner, reads

a gossip column. The top
of the salt shaker falls off
into the soup. The weight
of his bones speaks to him.

Each resides in the end
in a child's blue velvet box.
They rest comfortably in their new home,
while the chariot rises

and flies off in ever widening circles.

Michael Wurster

INHERITANCE

Who devises these seasons of knowing?
Roosevelt sat heads up, cigarette holder
clamped tightly between his teeth.
Young Kennedy ran into a tree.

Dreamt an argument with my daughter
in a maze of corridors leading
to a small space. Chaos on the stairs,
memories of wet paint in the Old Soldiers Home.

Pound in St. Elizabeth's. My father
in St. Elizabeth's. Olson enjoying
a country inn in Oxford, Maryland,
where I stayed several times years later,

the green lawn went right down to the water
of the bay. I feel a last child,
the one the sickle moon will cleanse.

OLD

The old wiggle their fingers at me,
grimace as I look down at them
in the ditch. Bald heads
or scraggly white hair. Comedy
indistinguishable from pain.

This is not a bottomless emptiness.
Happy porpoises jump in the sun.
The sky is an endless green.
The trees are drawn with crayons.

You sit in our past, mute,
and say, "Just. As near."

The inspector is Spanish, wears a white jacket.
A petrified nightingale falls off the table.
The lions are not mine.

Words batter the walls in an idea of flight.
You are prim and correct, wall us off.
The old try to climb, but the sides are too slick.

Michael Wurster

MY HEART

The drowsing Gorgons
lie fat in the grass.

The bones, when you find them,
will be dry and chalky.

My grandfather's legacy
shimmers before my eyes.

When I make love
the women shout.

My head is suspended
between two wires, my heart
fed to the lions and the wolves.

SARAJEVO 1970

for Radovan Karadzic

Misfortune marches
like an insect.

When time nears,
the insect will be crushed,
like the singer
crushed by silence
transforming him to sound.

This foretells mourning.

What is being prepared
in the garage
by that black metal?

Michael Wurster

HOT DAY ON THE NORTH SIDE

We saw a heavy-bearded guy
in a pink dress trying
to walk in high heels.
You said "the mysterious
helps us survive."

I said, "he's not mysterious,
he's just sad."

The postman peers through the mesh.
Is it a man or woman in there?
The day is red hot.

By the school it was
like a pep rally. The whole day
was a shimmering mess. A
voice like chocolate icing
called a name. The two women
turned, looked at us and smiled.

The drapes in the next window
were a rose color. The proprietor
was absent. As I write this,
the postman turns and moves on.

AGONISTE

for Hart Crane

A straw-thatched farmhouse
halfway up the mountain.
No electricity.

It's in the city
that the pretty boys
and aging men
lurch from lounge
to air-conditioned lounge.

Agoniste. Mouth open,
eyes wet, smiling,
back on the cross at dawn.

Michael Wurster

DISPLACED WORKER

He experiences heat at five.
"Oh-Oh, nowhere my beloved."
Blue wet. Innocence bleats,
a fly at the last,
hand, home, only an hour,
the envious weave,
the bridge of his life an Argentina.

He remembers Braniff, bright machines
that seemed to float.
Now, huddled and solitary, he eats grits
off a tin plate, the industrial plant
a catafalque of yesterday's prosperity,
sour and rotten,
a kind of harmony with the gray landscape of air.

A POTHOLE BIG ENOUGH
FOR A COFFIN

Charlie Samaha,
an actor from New Orleans,
an antique dealer from New York City,
a steel man, an investor in real estate,

Charlie Samaha,
with the neck of a bull,
a shaved head, mustachios,
a man you could not push over,

Charlie bought a coffin
and placed it in the pothole,
laid down in it like a dead man,

holding the stalk of an American flag
instead of a lily, this was
at rush hour on Friday afternoon.

On Saturday morning it was on the front page,
and on Monday city money
began to pour into the South Side.

Michael Wurster

KOSSOVO

Snick snack the butcher's back.
One murmurs of hoarders,
another describes her ordeal,

the leg gone, the foot
still in its shoe
in a basket in a truck

going the other direction,
passing soldiers
marching in the rain,

Willie and Joe,
the ghosts of Libya.

DEAD OR ALIVE

When I was a young man and desperate,
one day I got one bill too many,
wrote "DECEASED" on the envelope,
marched it down to the corner
and dropped it in the mailbox.

A half hour later a knock at the door,
the postman: "Michael,
you're either dead or alive.
If you're dead I have to return all your mail;
if alive you can't pick and choose."

Sadly I reached out my hand.

Michael Wurster

TRAVELING THROUGH OHIO
IN 1952

Conshohocken was a dirty town
then in winter. East Liverpool

was "across the alley from the Alamo."
The lines of the highway

were part of the pattern
of it all, moving. He didn't

really know what he was doing,
did anyone? You could sleep

in the back of a station wagon
in those days. At night

it was like a cave moving.
Agreement could come

with or without humiliation,
layers of impasto,

seven Indian tribes. By the end
of the century we'd be different people.

All the chairs would be forgotten,
moved back for dancing. Let's

forget together, waltzing through
the lovely rooms, bandages over our eyes.

A BEGINNING

for Judy

1.

How it rains once
when we walk together in Pittsburgh,
we think it is always so.

The rain/water is received
by the bricks and sidewalks.

Like red earth, good black loam.

Like this.

2.

How we dance to the jazz
from the radio at night
on Bedford Square, guessing

the tunes, every moment
a moment of grace.

Michael Wurster

TEABAGS ARRANGED DIFFERENTLY

1.

The map room
Vienna Austria 1938
I'll never forget
George Raft
on that windowledge
outside the building
above the streets
listening.

2.

I'll never forget
the wind blowing
thru your hair
as the 39 feet
danced.

It was the first image
we saw
when we awoke.

ELECTION

My poems have become dangerous.
My poems have holes sewn onto them.
They surround the White House.
They are the armies of the night.

I am a peaceful man from Moline.
My black pearls are the oysters
in your Christmas stocking.
You can see them on television.

Wait for the rusted trains
where the poet's eye capsizes.
I have a friend in a white suit.
He wears a black diamond in his lapel.

Under the sunken light I build,
a poet in chains. The pull of the earth
that the skydivers love. Cities
are in flames. Whatever is left

of memory? The old sorrow.

Michael Wurster

INTIMIDATED BY THE BREAKAGE

No purple open. Eyes alone.
Skin jumps. I should tell them.
The foliage is covered
with cloth during the night.

No place like home
to disturb the evidence.
By mid-morning a weak light
tires the pictures.

BRAKHAGE

Painstaking events in real time.
Creeley crossing his legs.
Proclamations from darkness, order.
The meaning of the hand:

the hand reminding in the pasture,
the hand without a crack on the shelf,
the hand in the garden of practice,
charged and shimmering.

I love to watch you walk
across the room, your clothing
white, or black. The motif of rain.

POEM ABOUT AMERICA

In Clinton Iowa
on the Mississippi

there's a small ballpark,
Riverfront Park.

The team is called the Pilots.

The home run balls
go into the water
and down to New Orleans.

YOUR DONKEY

Military troops bear witness
to the sadness of the day.

The cymbals burn black.
The leaves petrify and, like glass,

make a hell of a noise
when they fall from the trees.

Your donkey won't go there again.

Michael Wurster

THE INVISIBLE EMPIRE

Dance and weave, build and ride,
always more. Eclipse,

love letter from the past,
the screams my ears have heard.

Rub a dub tub, evil in the drain.
Men sit on porches, waiting.

The evening sky is crimson,
but later the syllables

will burn up on the ridge.

CHILD

As a child he prayed to God,
mysterious innocence of need.

No embarrassment then. All
the hours, the sun rising

and setting as if it were natural,
almost casual. He walked

through the fields into old rooms.
Books were piled on each table.

He'd forgotten something,
an injury from the train wreck?

And in the mirror, a crucifix
of black. The stars relent,

test the heart's railing.

Michael Wurster

THOSE MISSING TOWERS

Sartre said it's easy to
describe a presence, but hard
to define an absence.

On September 12, 2001,
New York City defines an absence
as a hole in the heart,

those missing towers in the skyline.

VAUCLUSE

for René Char

Before I could call myself by my true name,
the bird sang and was gone. One feather.

When day withdraws to the ends of the earth,
the nimble torches of the mind surface again.

Within your kindness my anguish grows.
Ancient instruments oppose your acclimatized eyes.

There are worse things in our lives, always.
The fruit is ripe. Flies and ghosts are kept out.

I am not on the point of death.
All this transparency pushes time back.

What I lost was the immeasurable sun.
How could I have let it get away?

Michael Wurster

CONVERSATION WITH JUL

"What did I always tell you? What?

I said, don't get caught napping.
Don't let them catch you napping.

And what happens? I open
the newspapers

and there you are."